The Magic
of
Snow

Snow Scenes Of The Hudson Valley New York

Kathleen G. Morrissey

To order additional copies of this book, contact:
Xlibris Corporation
1-888-795-4274
www.Xlibris.com
Orders@Xlibris.com

Kathleen G. Morrissey is a graduate of the State University
of New York at Cobleskill. She enjoys photography and
raising horses in Dutchess County New York.

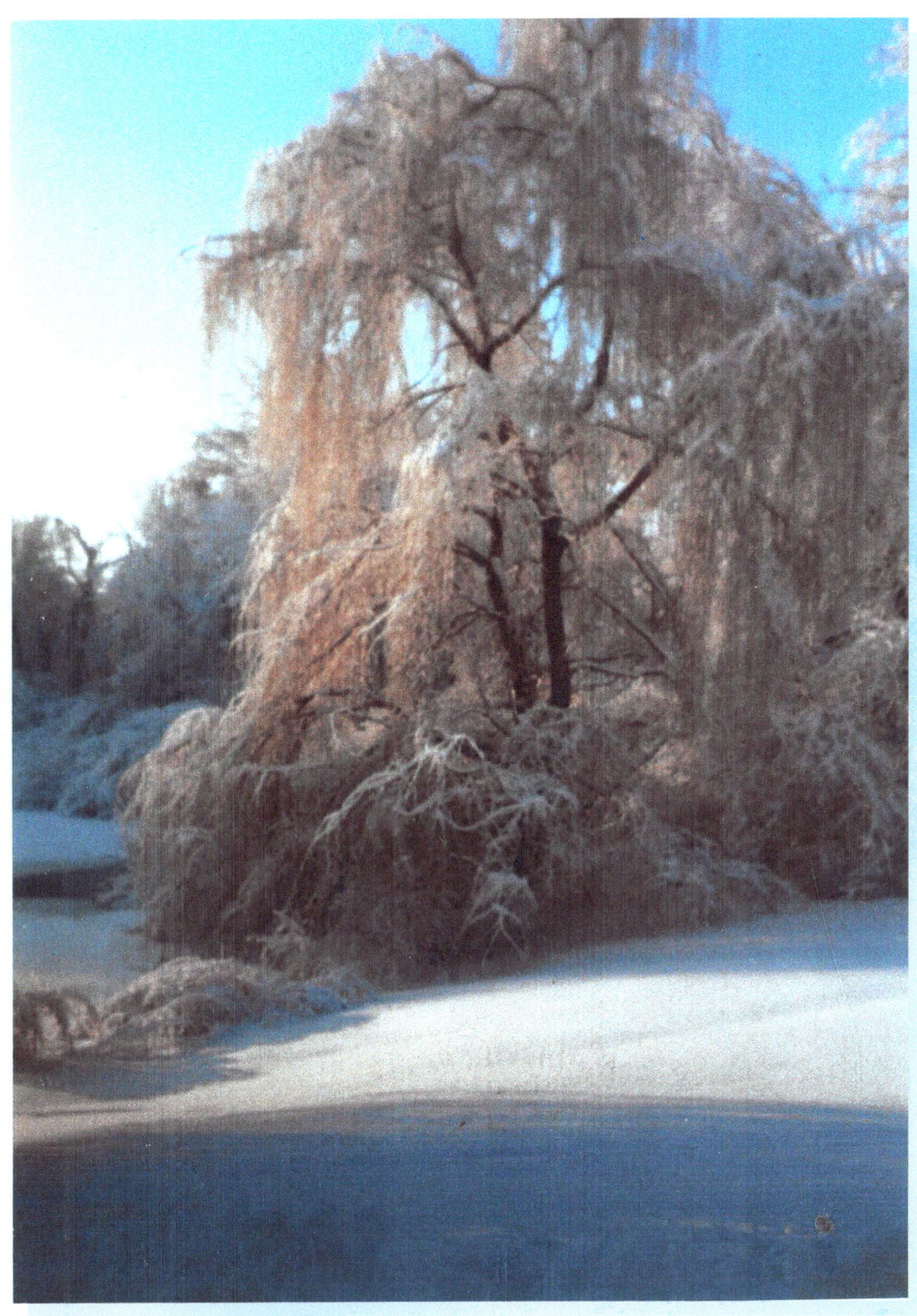

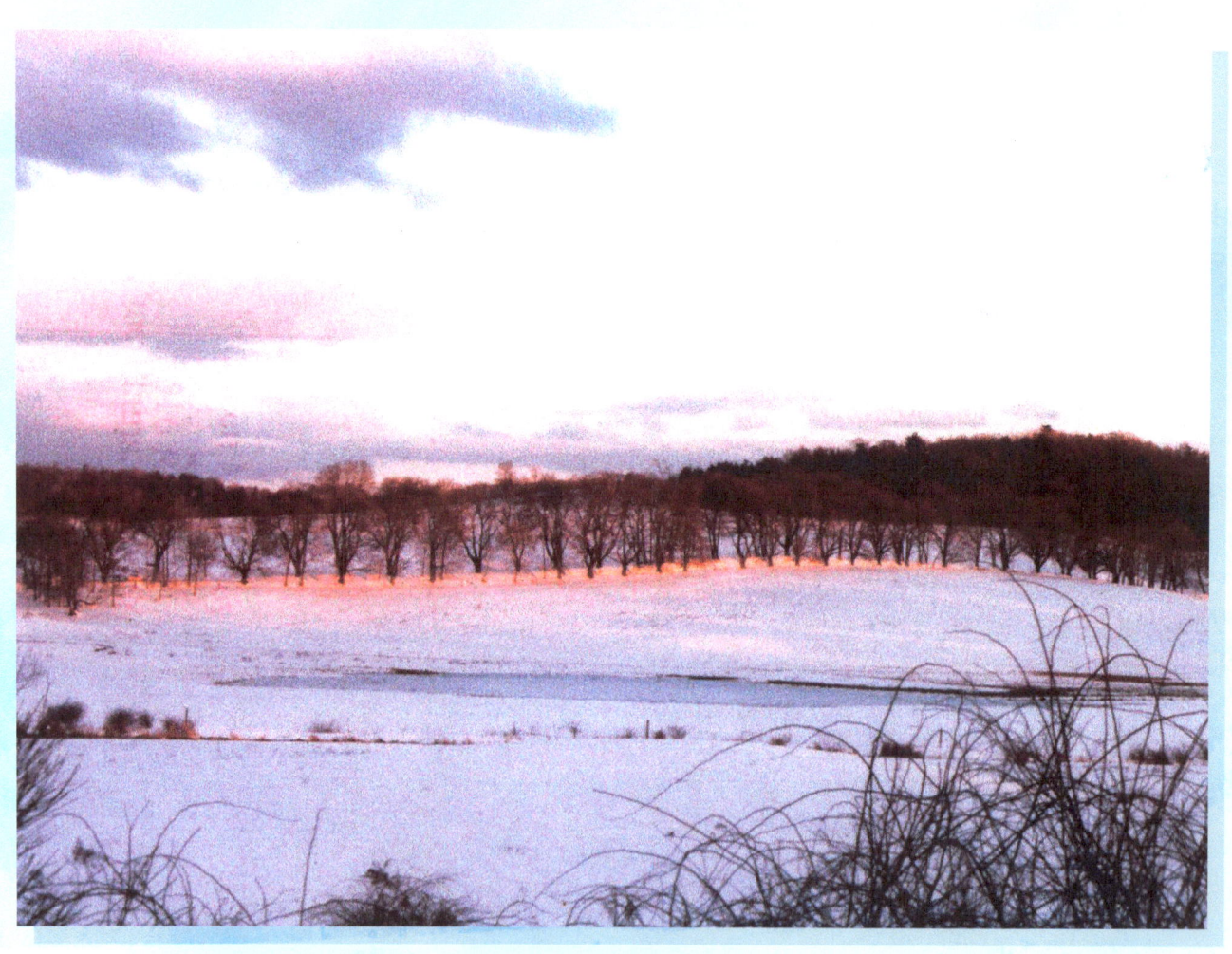

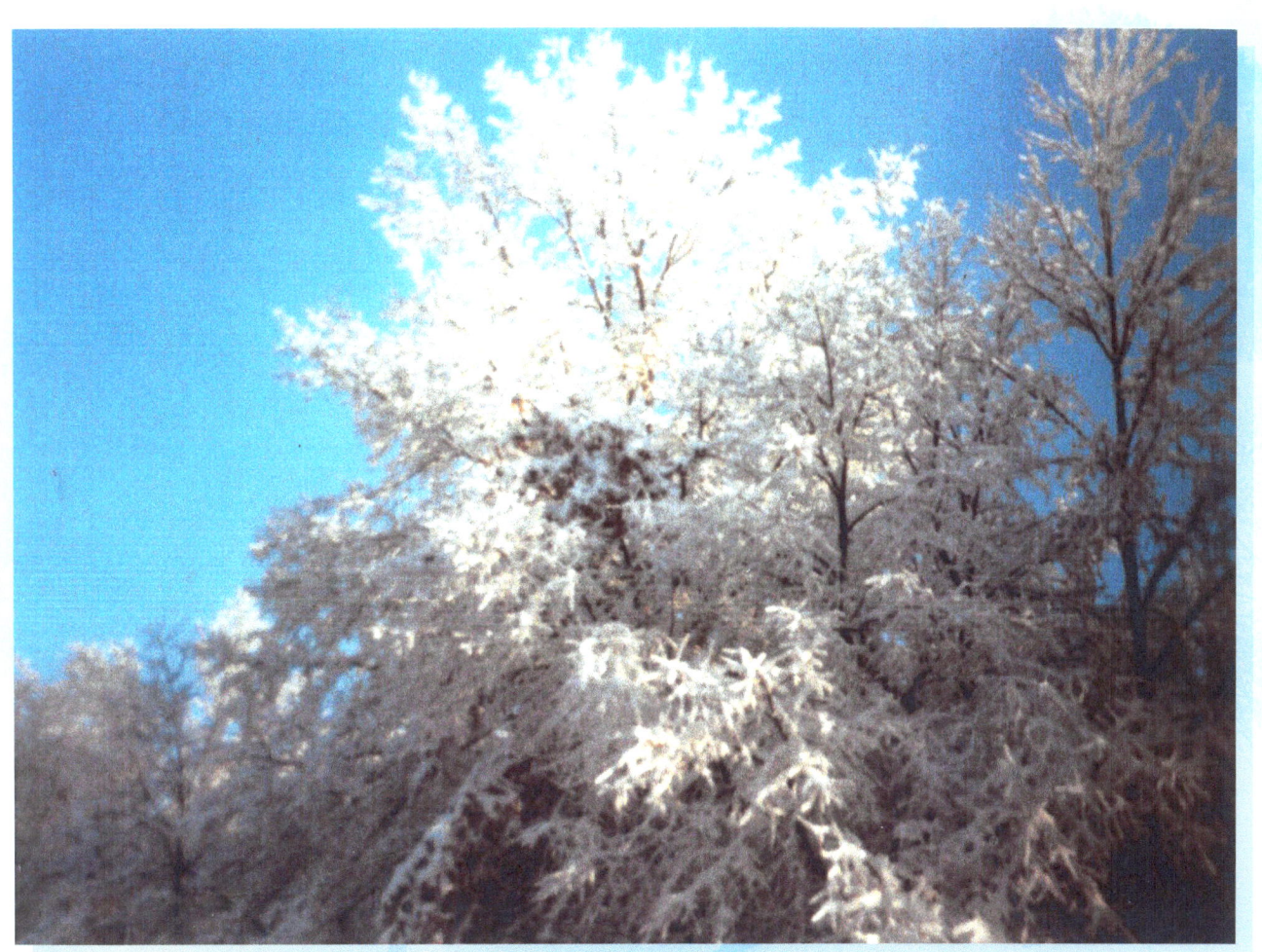

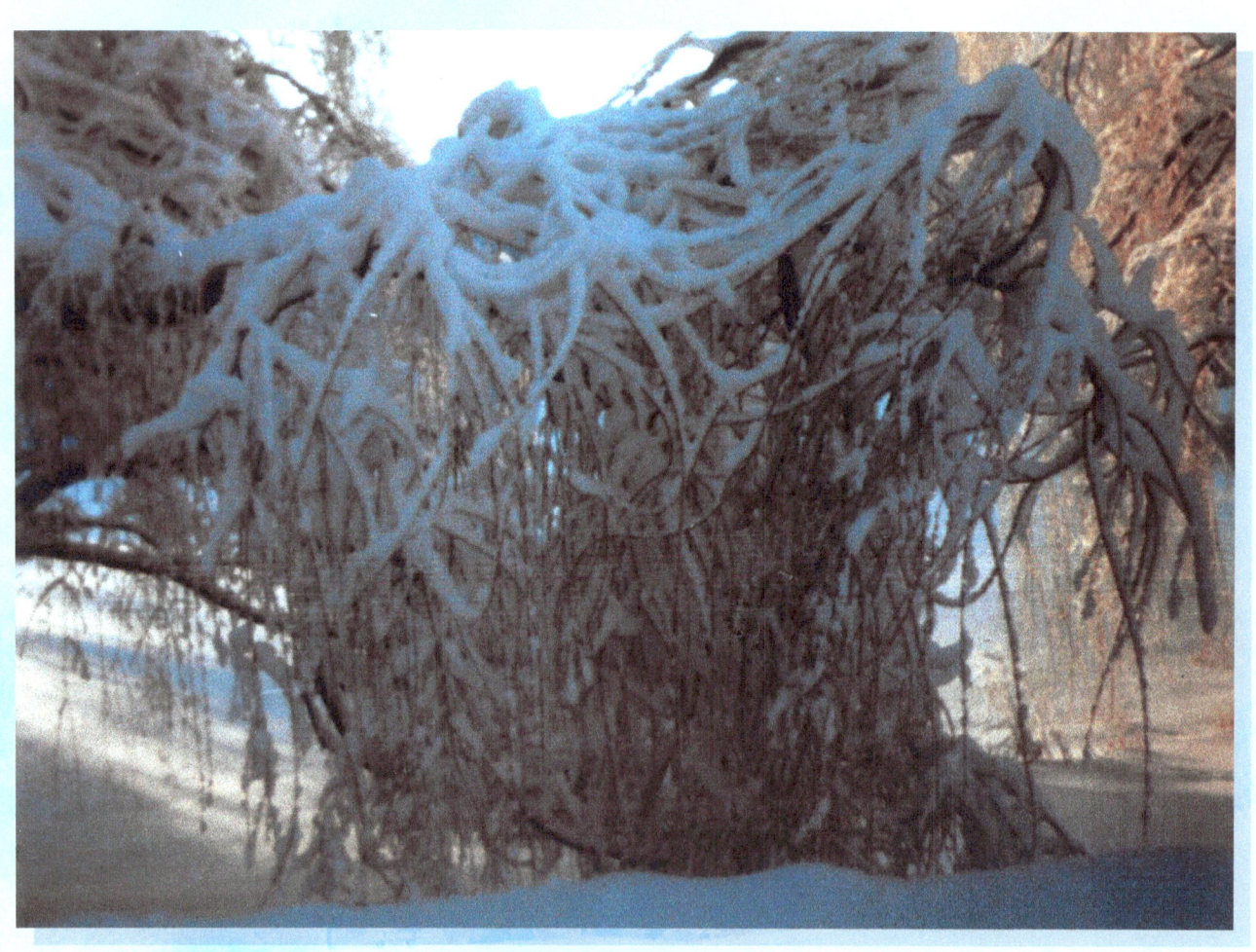

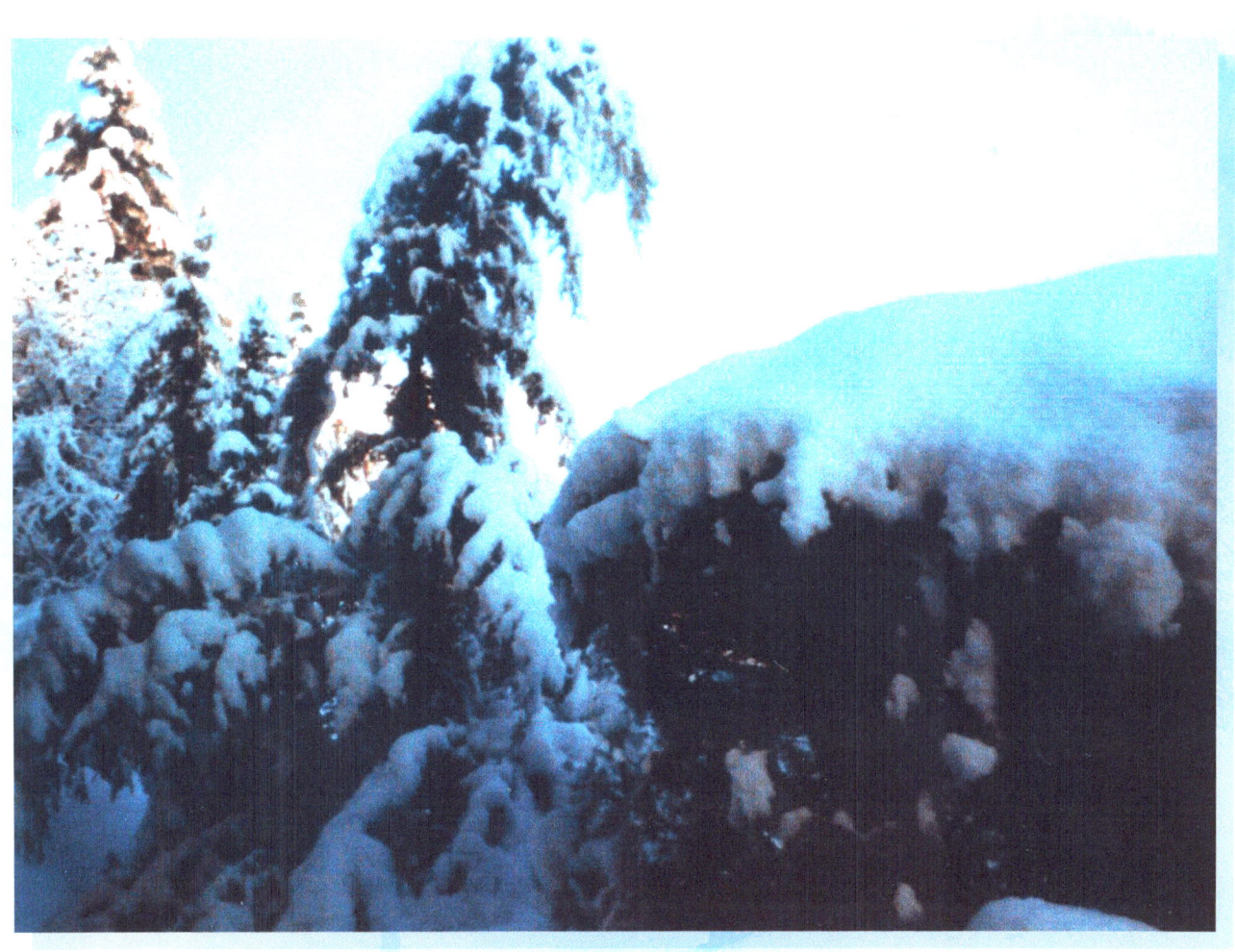

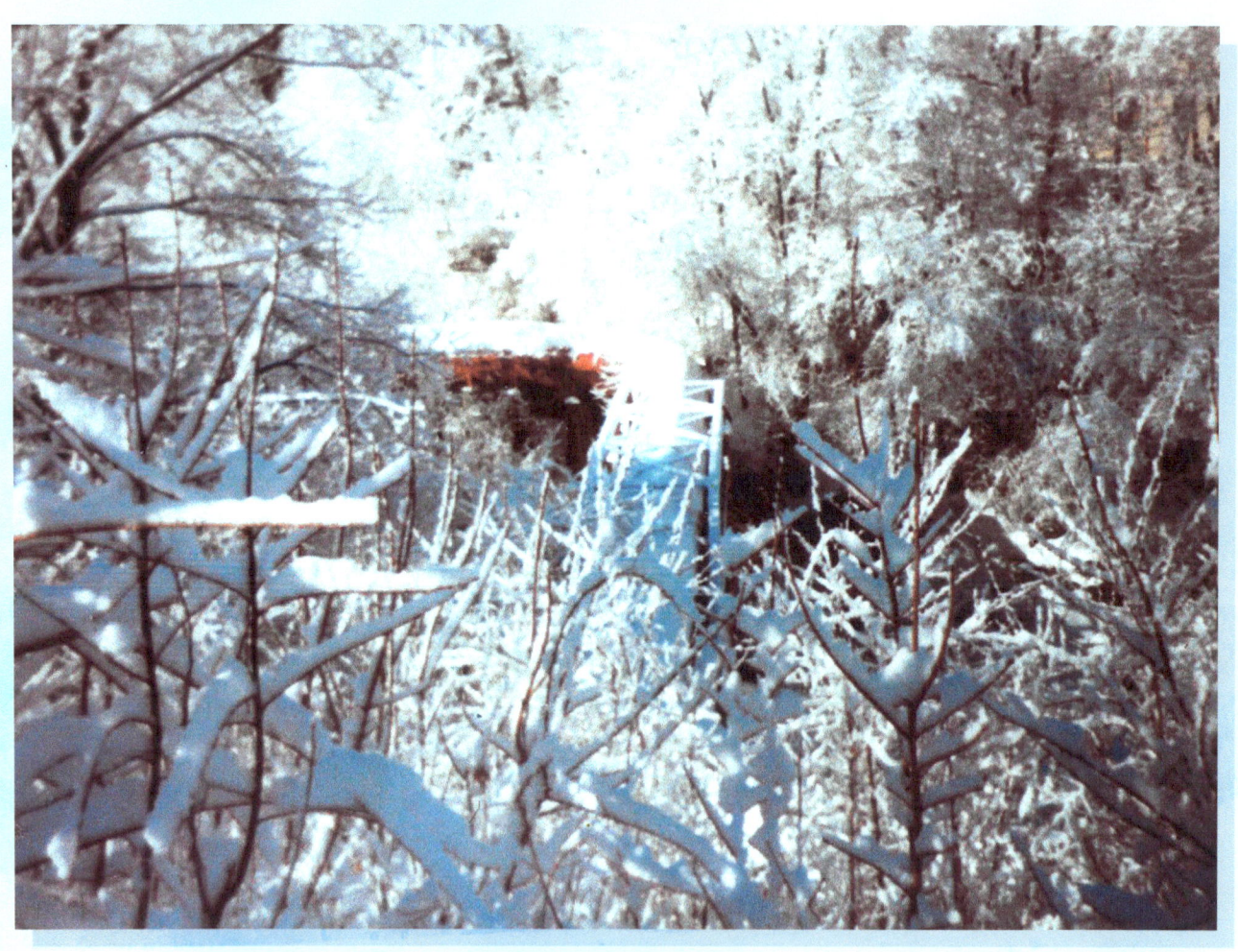

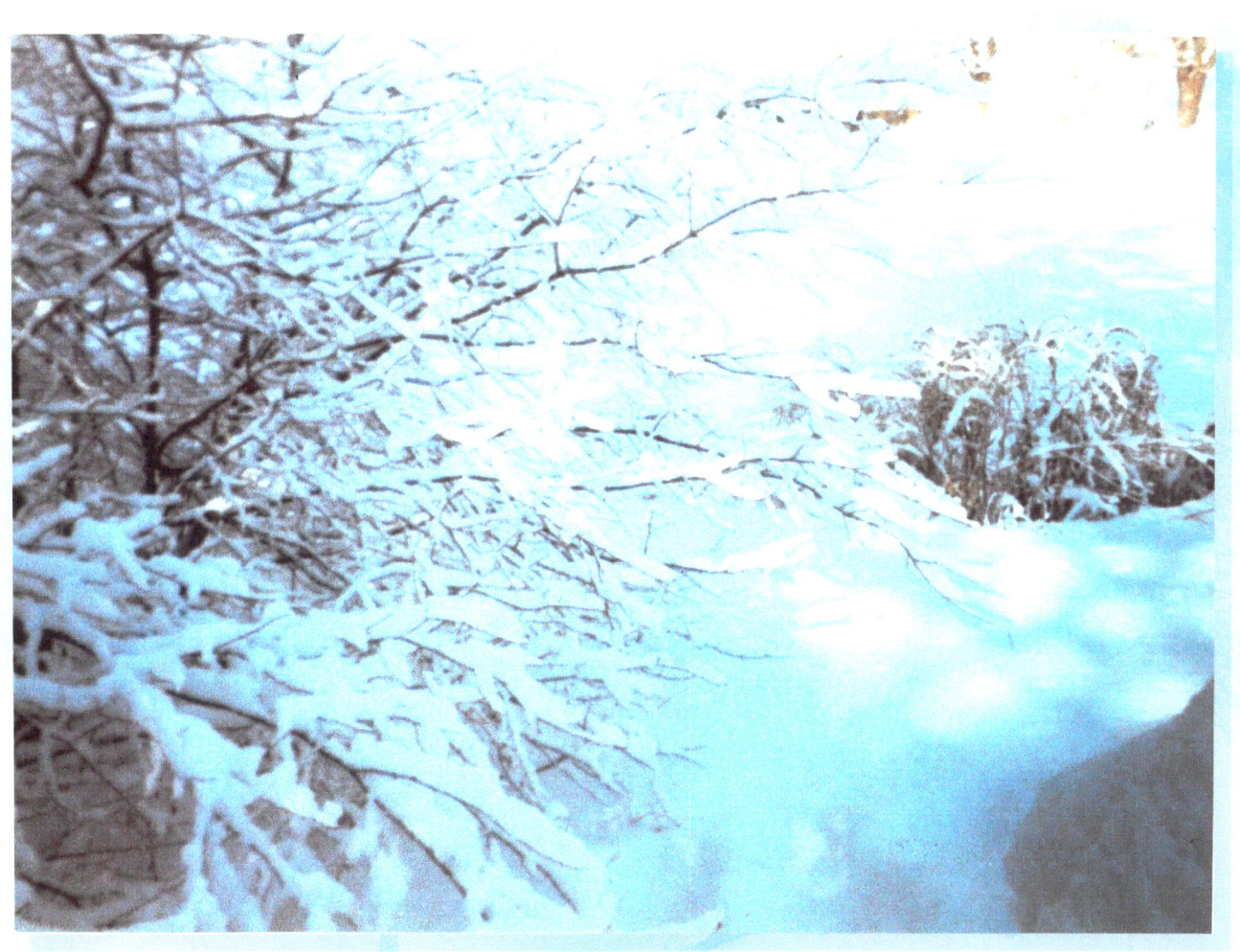

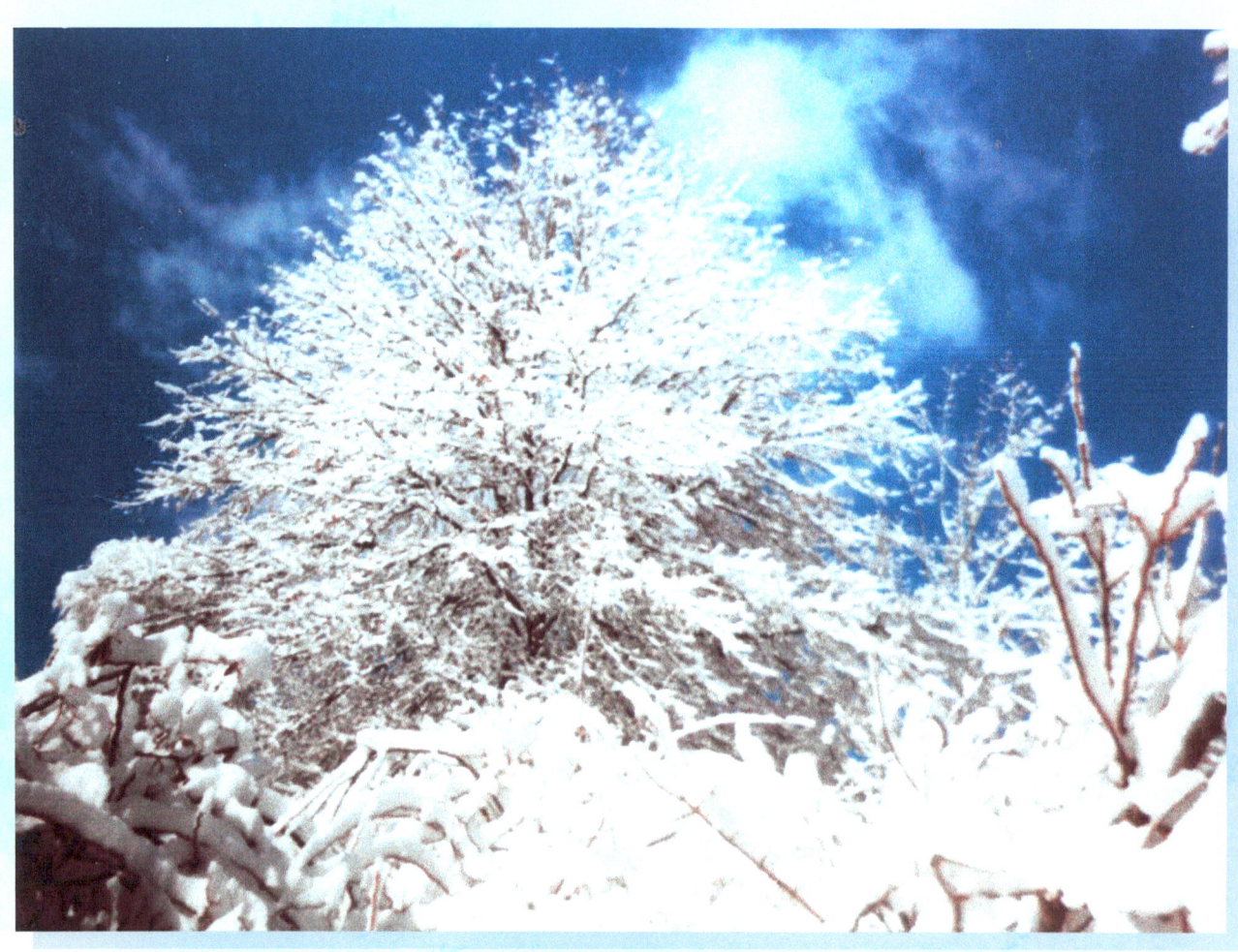

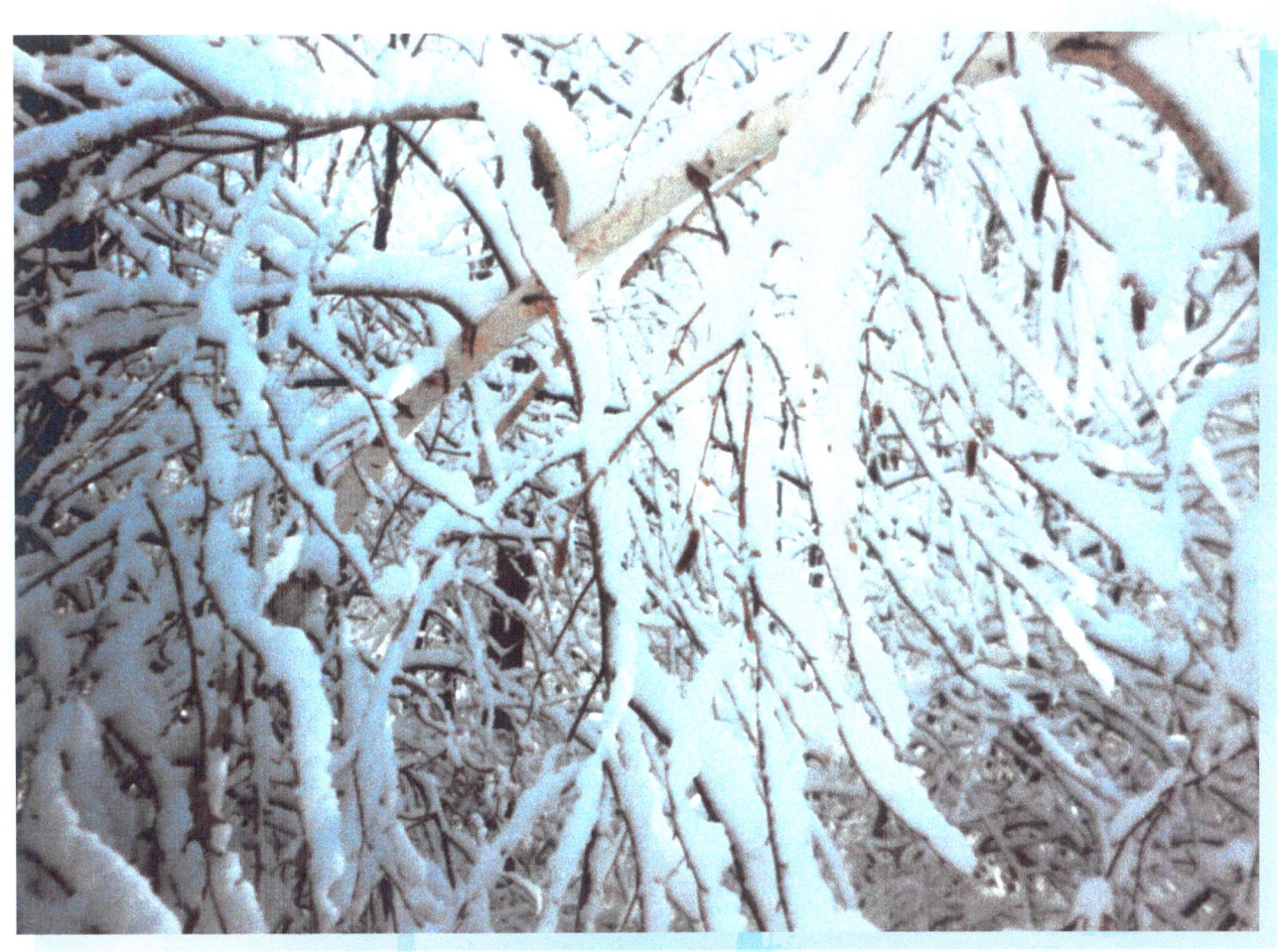

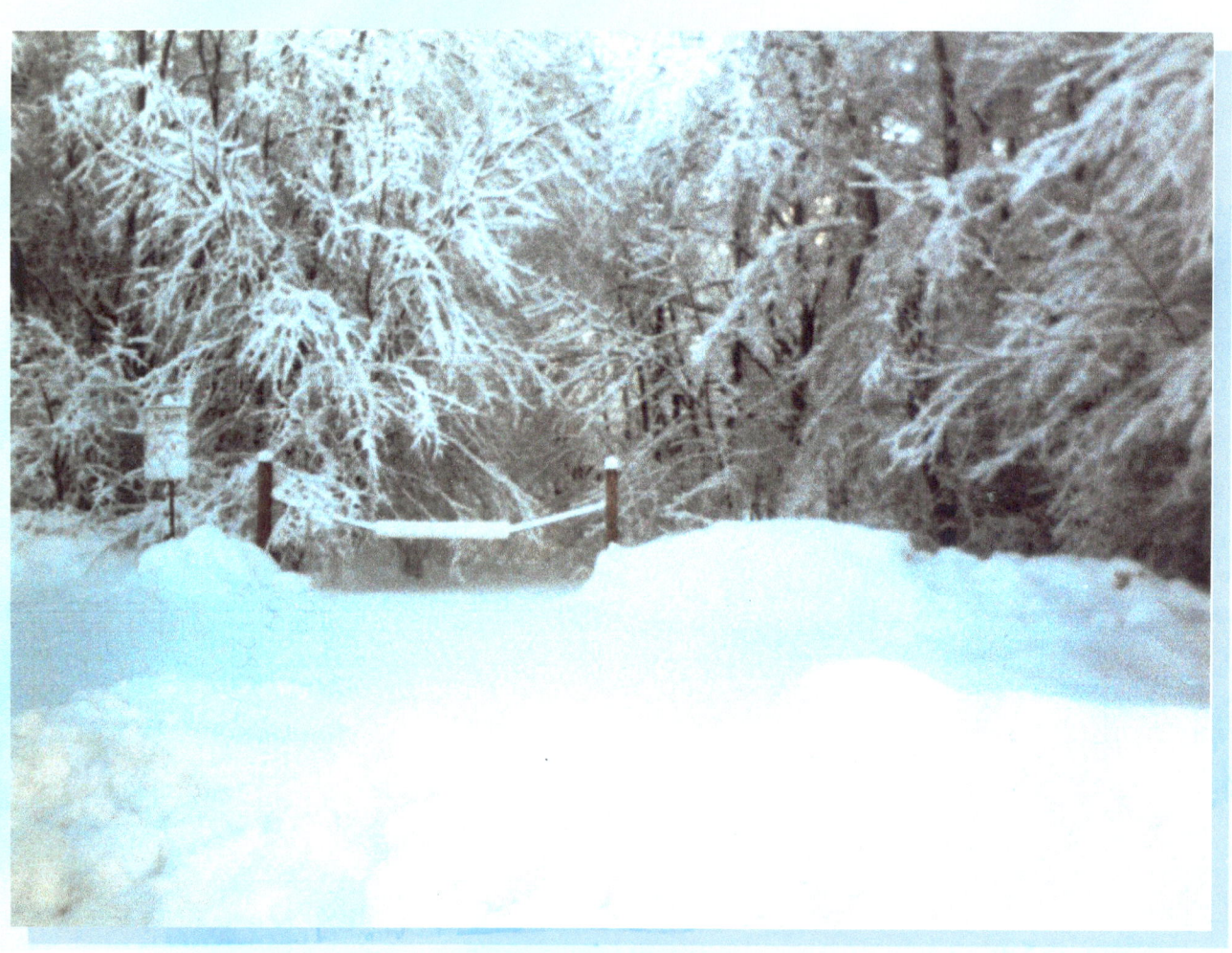

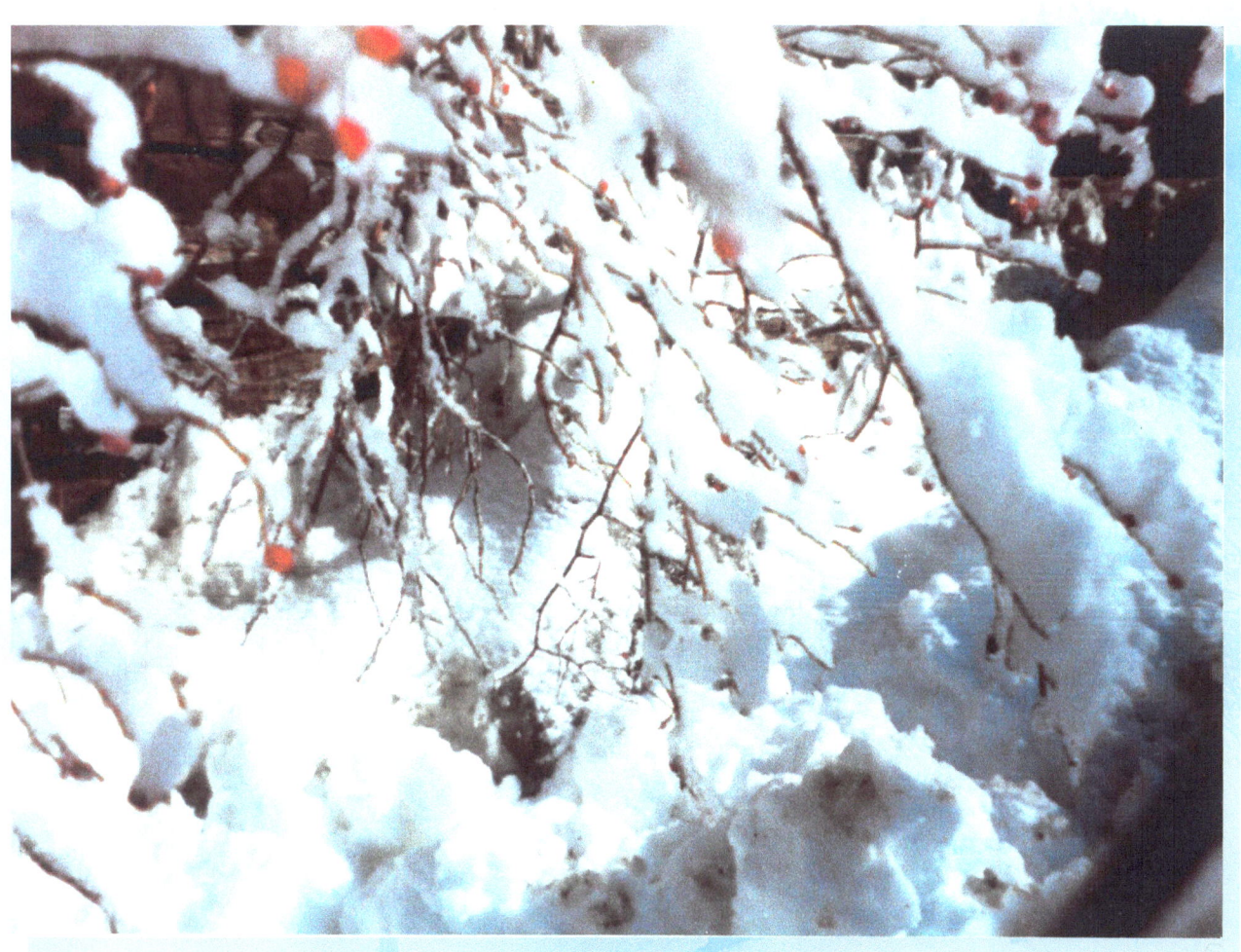

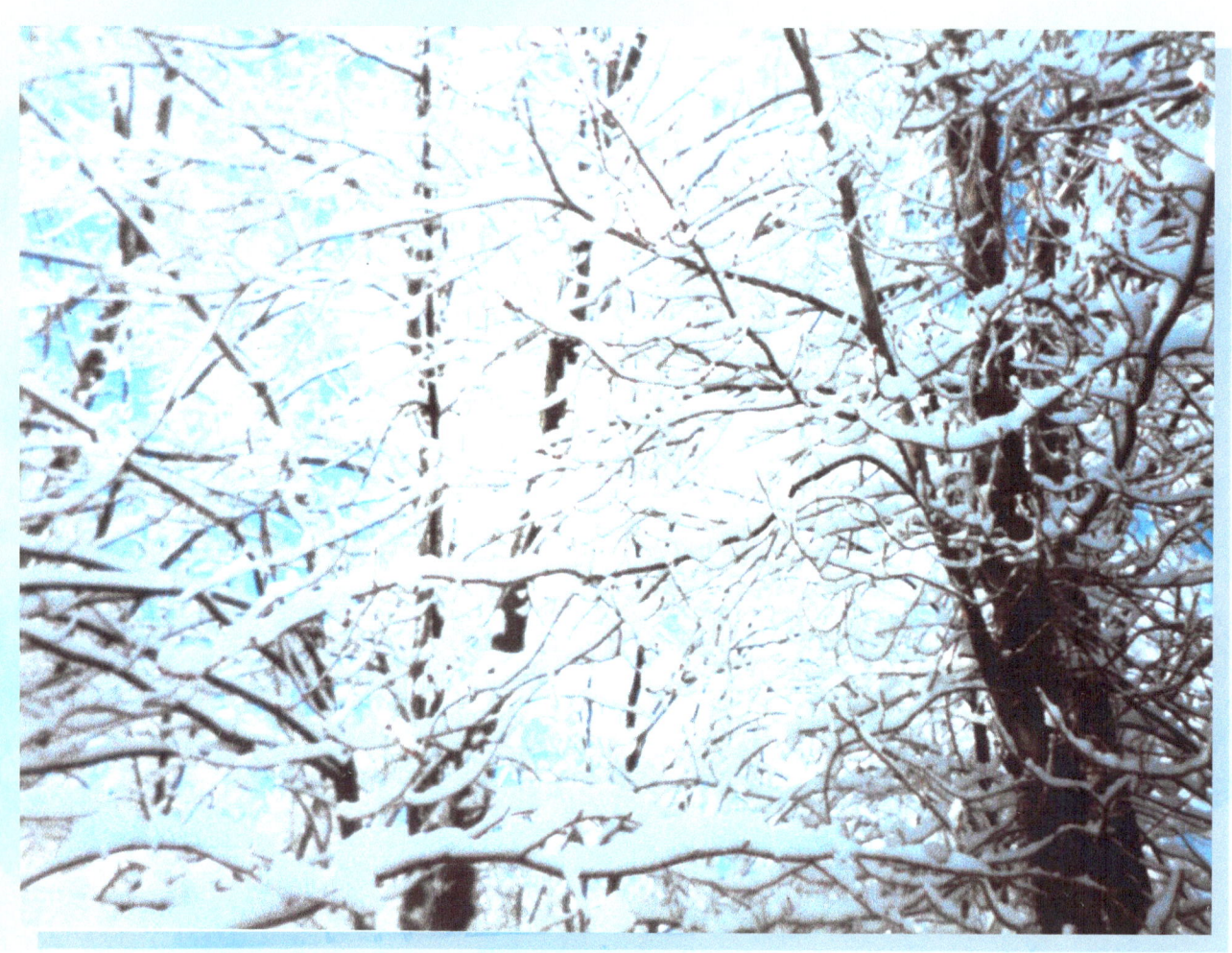

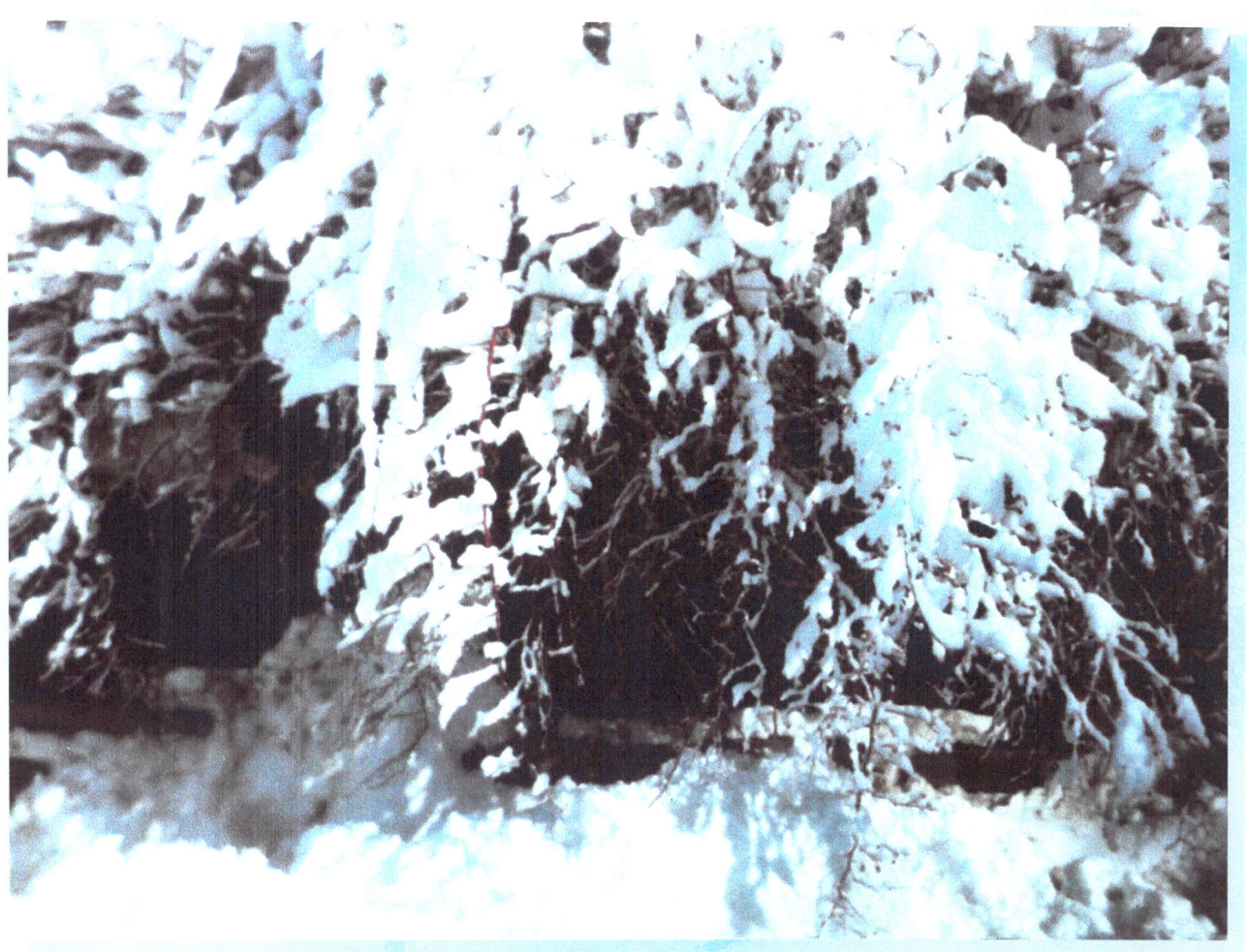

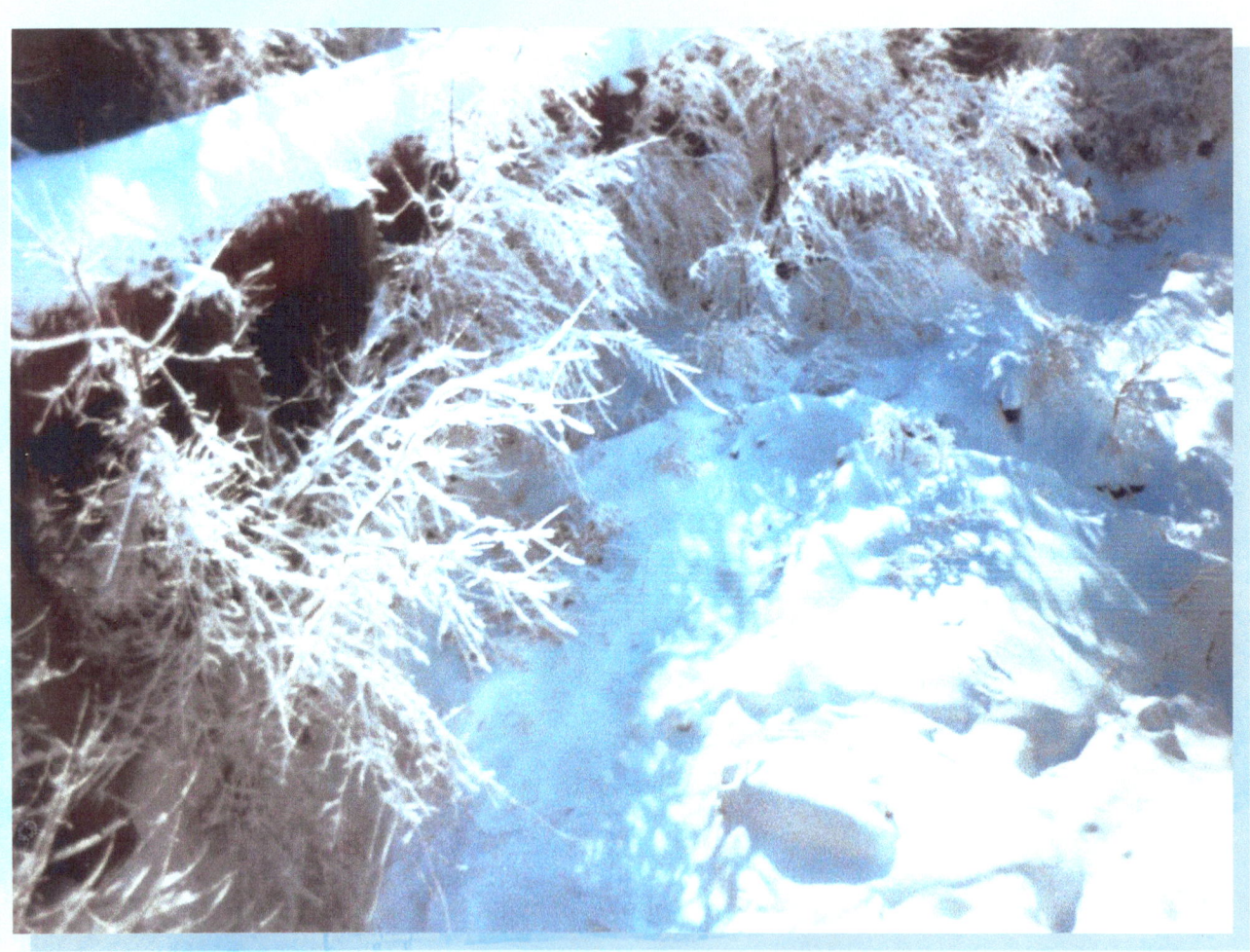

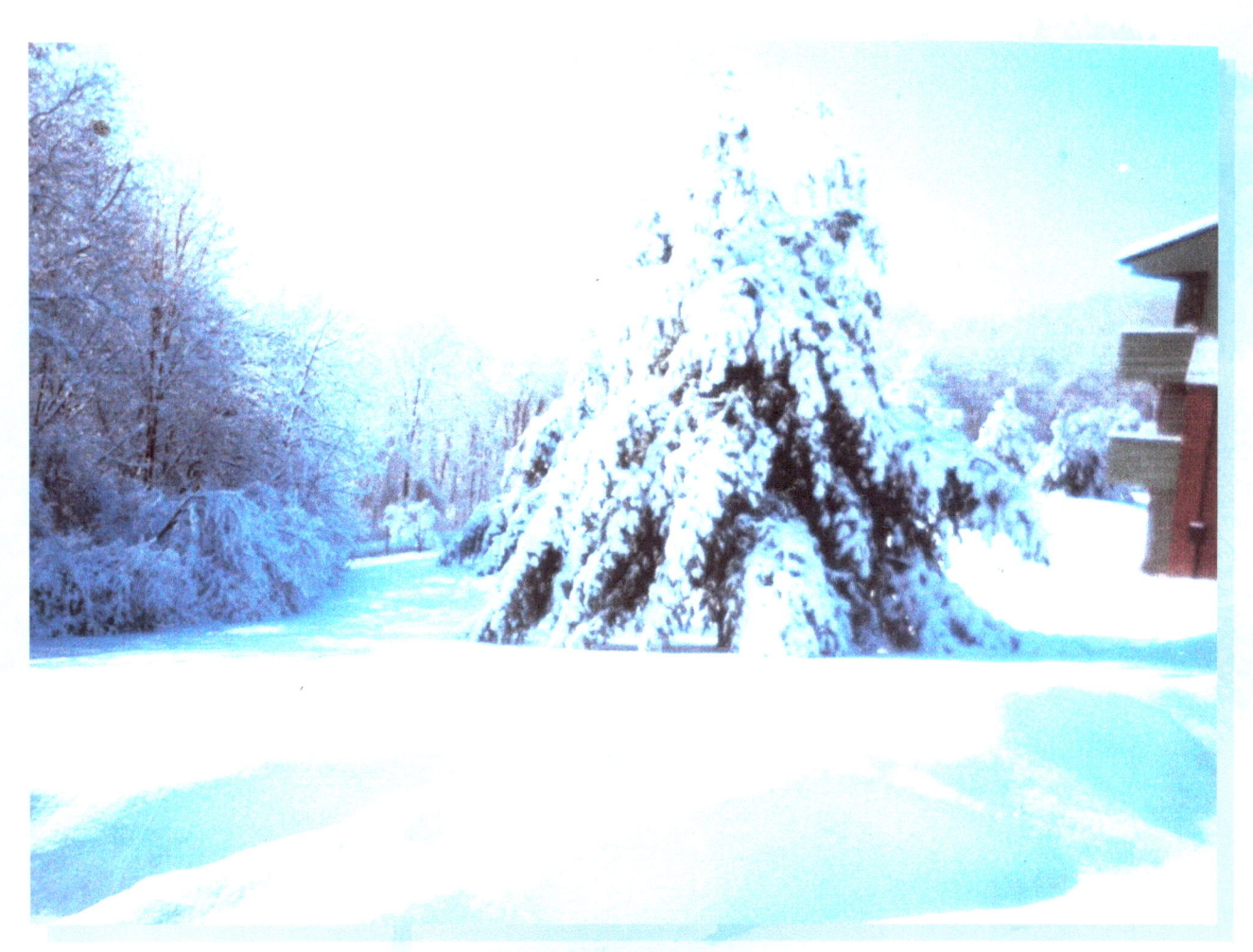

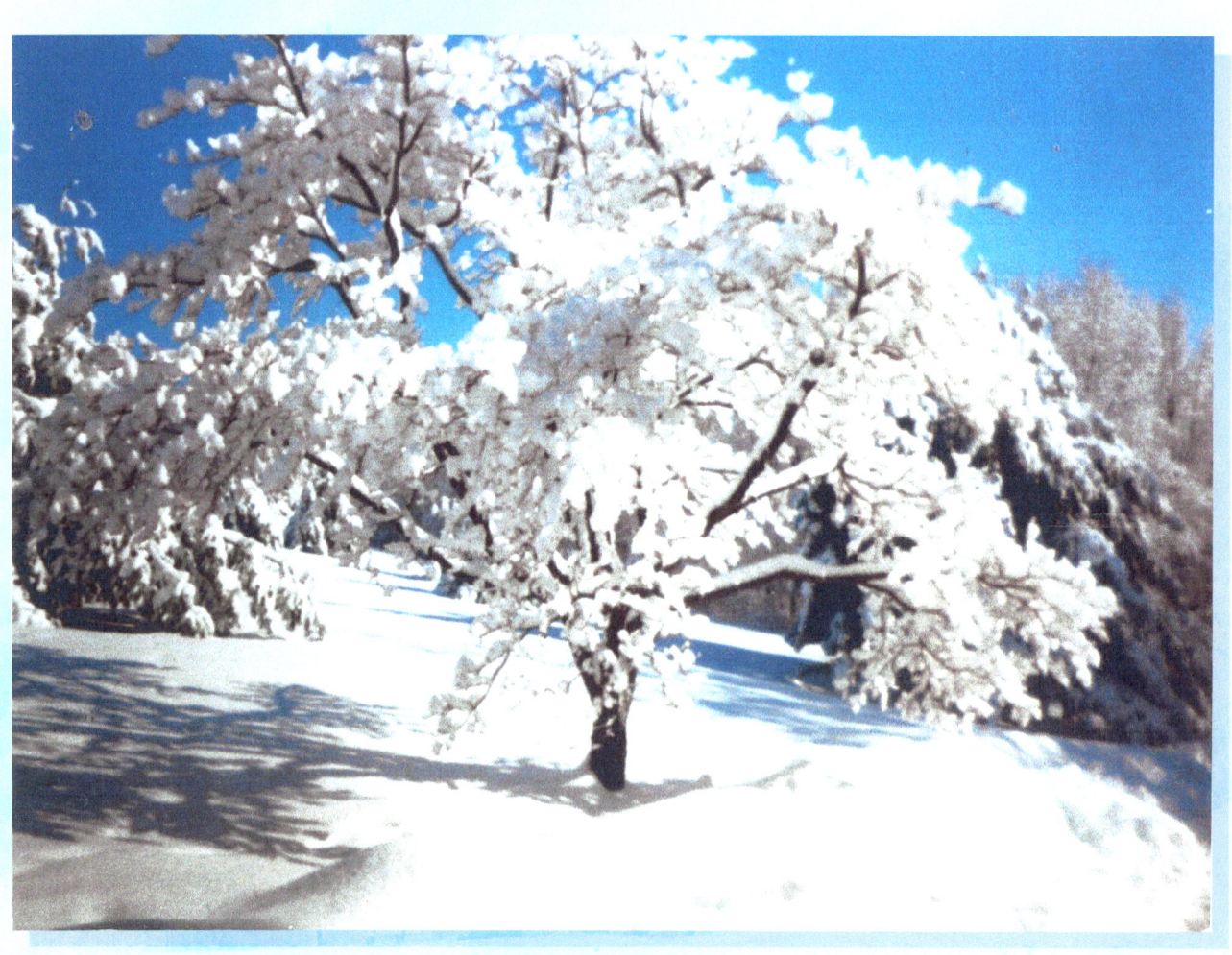

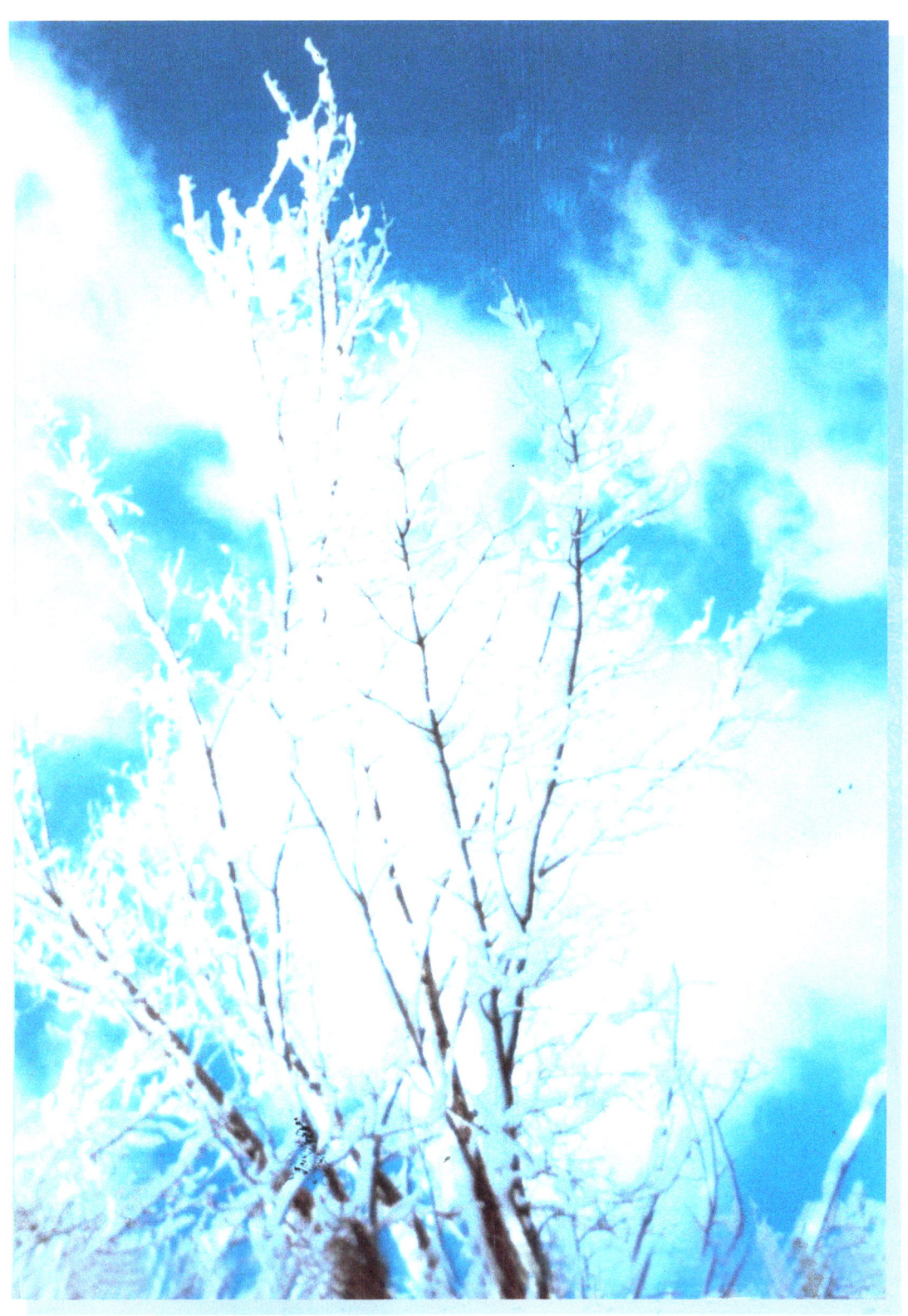

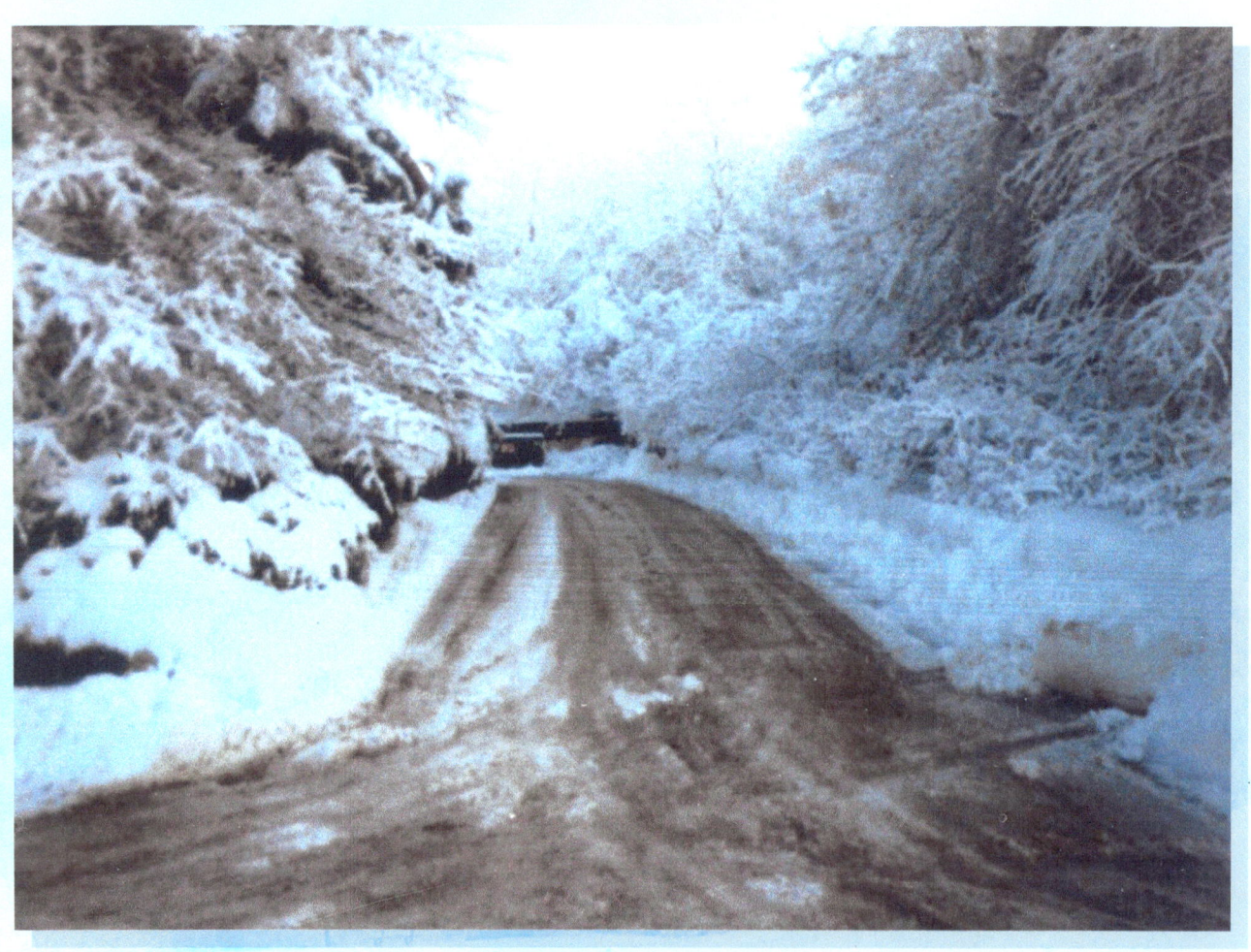

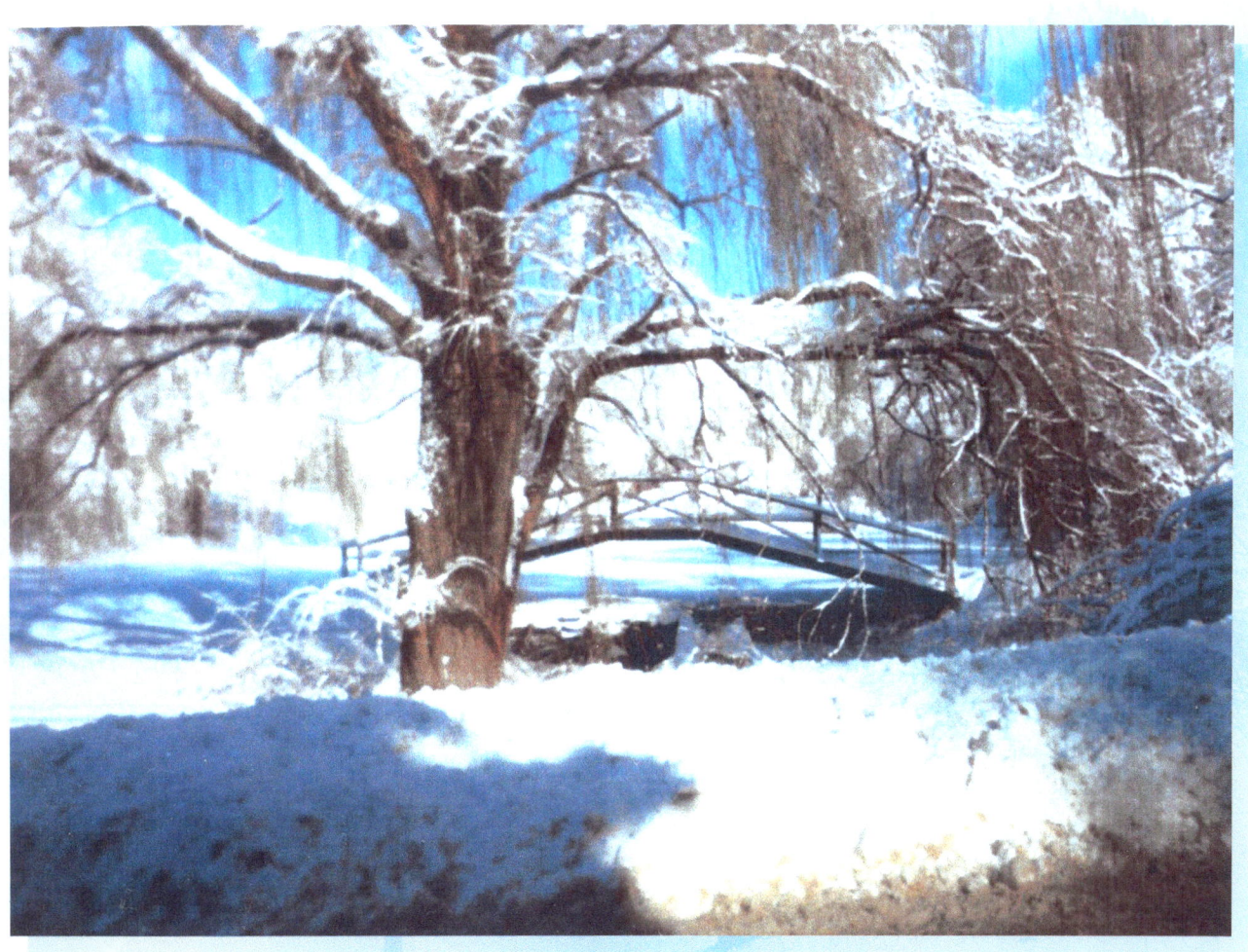

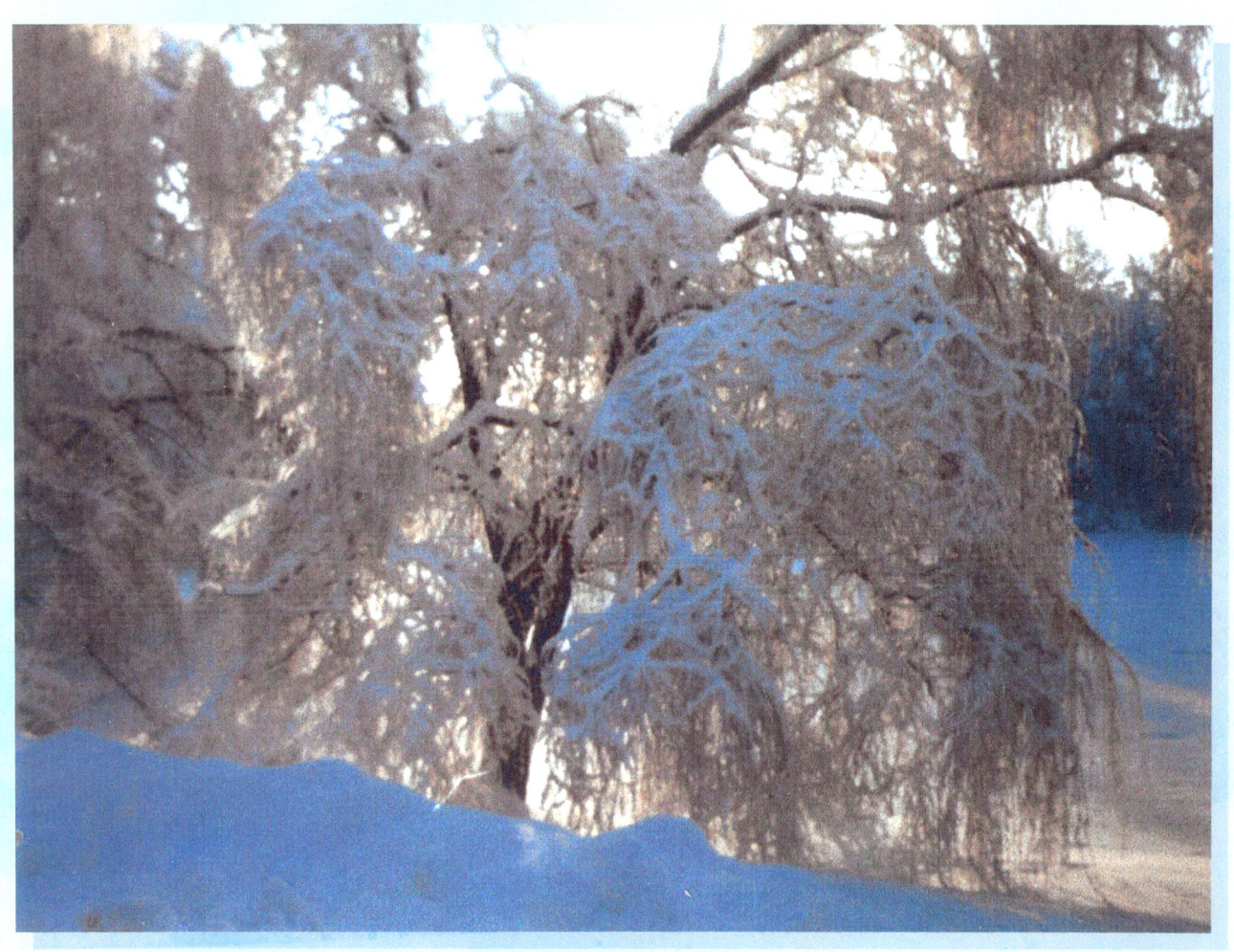

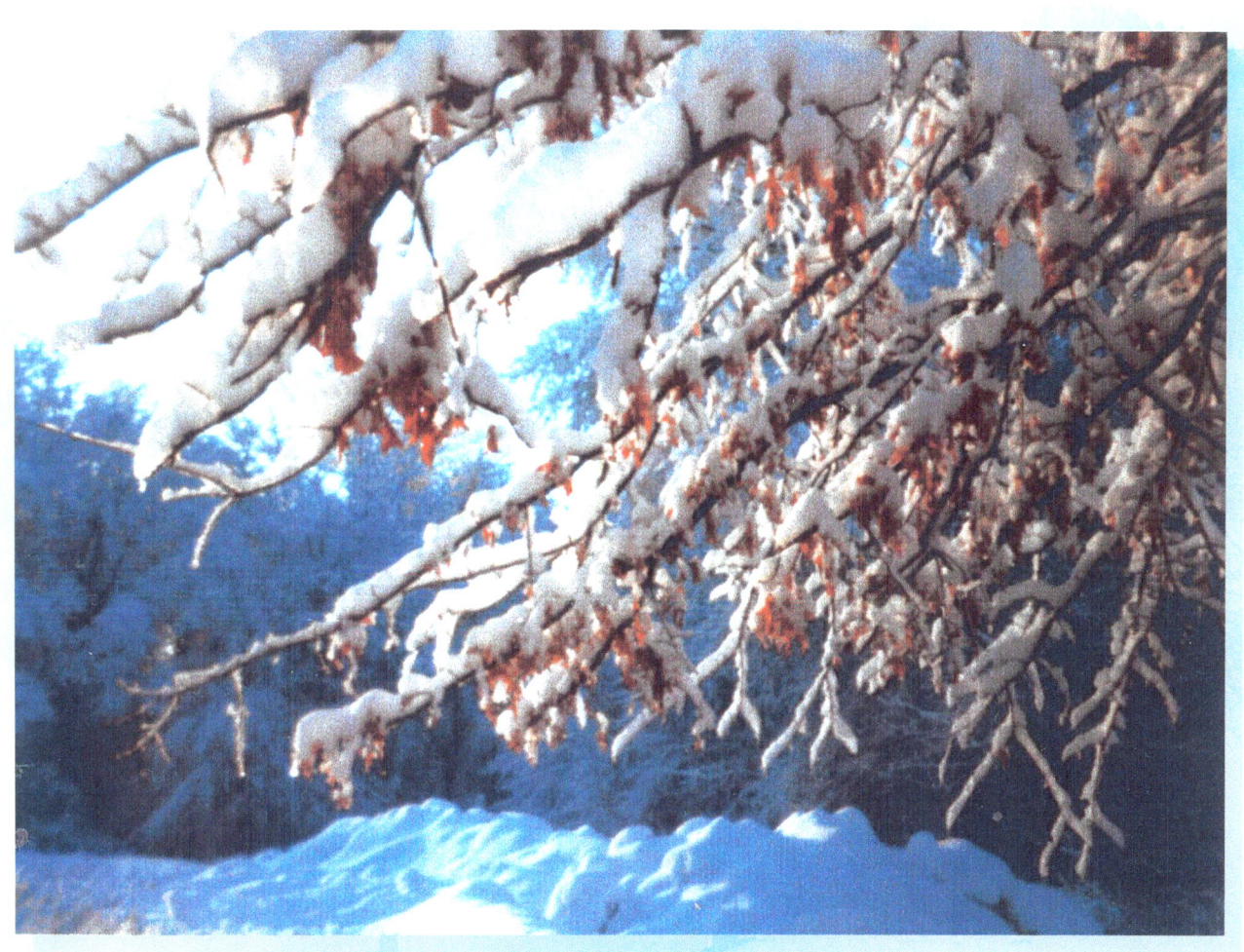

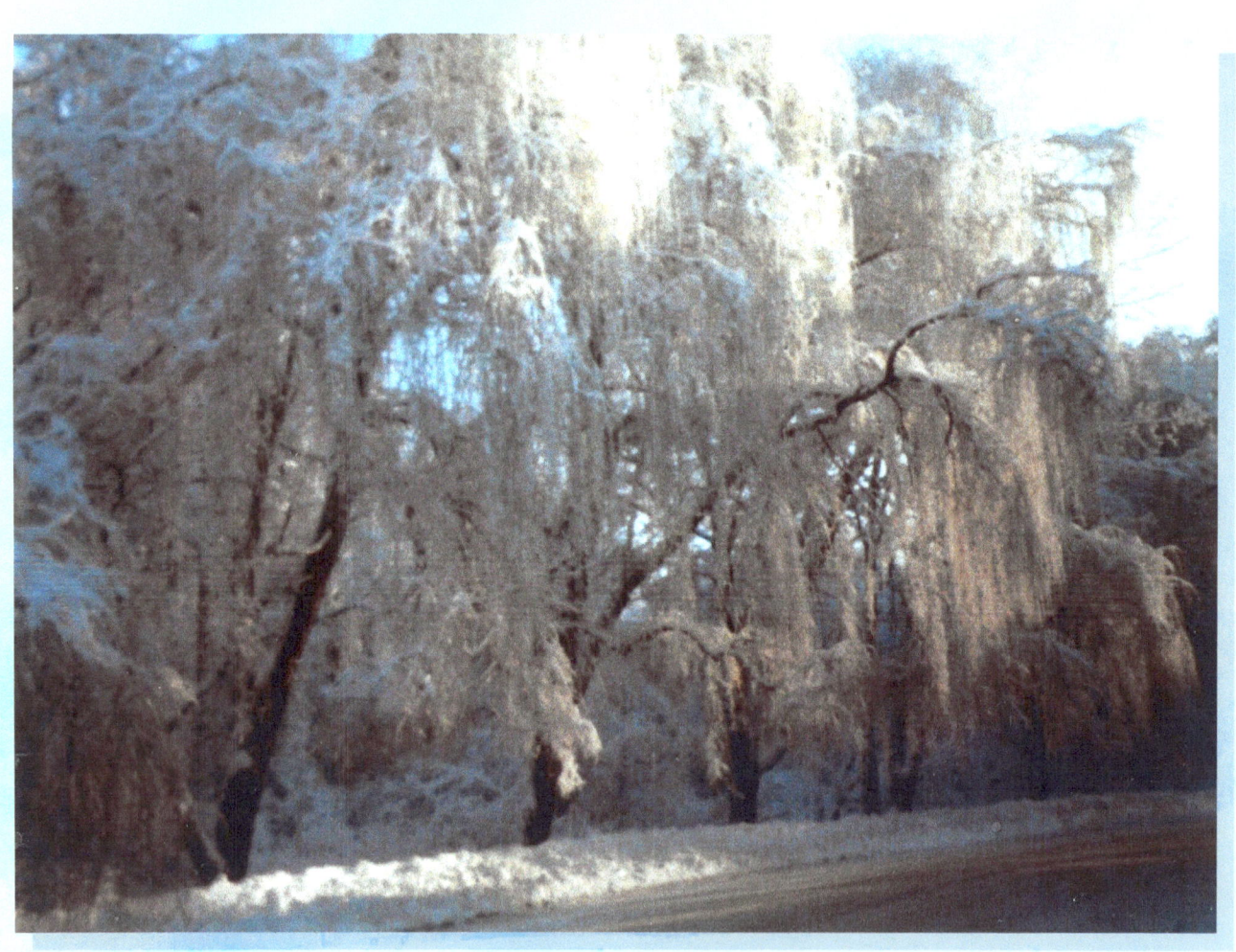